Faithful Servant Series
Meditations for New Members

June J. McInerney
Christopher L. Webber, Series Editor

MOREHOUSE PUBLISHING

Anglican Book Centre
Toronto, Canada

Morehouse Publishing   **Anglican Book Centre**
P.O. Box 1321   600 Jarvis Street
Harrisburg, PA 17105   Toronto, Ontario, Canada M4Y2J6

Morehouse Publishing is a division of The Morehouse Group.

Printed in the United States of America

Cover design by Corey Kent

Library of Congress Cataloging-in-Publication Data

McInerney, June J.
    Meditations for new members / June J. McInerney.
        p.   cm. — (Faithful servant series)
    ISBN 0-8192-1821-9 (pbk. : alk. (paper)
        1. New church members—Prayer-books and devotions—English.
    2. Episcopal Church—Government—Meditations.
    I. Title. II. Series.
    BV4596.N48M35   1999
    242'.69—dc21   99-37583
                              CIP

*For Dennis and Helen, Kirsten, Shirlee,
MaryBeth, Pat, Dorothy, Linda and Steve, Frankie, Clare,
and all the saints of Epiphany*

———"You Were Chosen"———

Were you chosen to read this book? Perhaps it was given to you in a public ceremony or maybe it was handed to you with a quiet "you might like to look at this." Maybe, on the other hand, it reached out to you in a bookstore and said, "Buy me!" Many books choose us in such ways and this book is likelier to have done so than most. But however this book came to you, it almost certainly happened because you have also been chosen for a ministry in the church or for church membership. Perhaps you hadn't considered this as being chosen; you thought you decided for yourself. But no, you were chosen. God acted first, and now you are where you are because God took that initiative.

God acts first—the Bible is very clear about that and God acts to choose us because God loves us. And who is this God who seeks us in so many ways, who calls us from our familiar and comfortable places and moves us into new parishes and new roles? Christians have been seeking answers to that question for a long time.

Part of the answer can be found within the church. We come to know God better by serving as church members and in church ministries. God is present with us and in others all around us as we worship and serve. But there is always more, and God never forces a way into our hearts. Rather, God waits for us to be quiet and open to a deeper relationship.

And that's what this book is about. This is not simply a book to read but to use, in the hope that you will set aside some time every day for prayer and the Bible—and for this book. So give yourself time not only to read but to consider, to think about, to meditate on what you have read. The writers of these short meditations have been where you are, thought about their experiences deeply, and come to know God better. Our prayer is that through their words and experience and your reflection on them, you will continue to grow in knowledge and love—and faithful service—of this loving, seeking God.

— Christopher L. Webber
   Series Editor

─────── Introduction ───────

You are probably reading this because you've just recently joined or rejoined a church. Whatever your reasons, it is a daunting experience, isn't it? As a newcomer, you are probably running the gamut of emotions, from being somewhat anxious to being excited, eager, and even joyous. The prospect of learning about and openly sharing your faith with others, especially strangers, can be intimidating. But it doesn't have to be. I know. I've been there, exactly where you are now. And I have had some of the same thoughts and feelings you are thinking and experiencing right now, as well as some of the same questions: Is this the right church for me and for my family? Am I doing everything correctly? Will I be accepted? Will the other members like me? Will I like them?

There is so much to learn, to be a part of, that as a newcomer you might feel a little overwhelmed. There were moments for me when I thought of not attending the following Sunday. But, as you will discover in these pages, something nudged me to go back, week after week. Before I knew it, I was no longer a newcomer but an established member welcoming others.

Because of family moves, career changes, and a few major life passages, I've been a new member of a congregation eight times in my journey. Most of them were not easy transitions. Some were exciting, one or two quite frightening, while others were more enjoyable. All of them, however, were opportunities for change and growth in spiritual awareness, as I matured in my faith as a living member of the inestimable community of the Body of Christ that you are now joining.

Because this growth and change is so important to me, I wish to humbly share my experiences, thoughts, and reflections with you. I hope that reading these meditations will facilitate your transition into the church. Perhaps they will help you be more confident and secure as you take these first tentative steps on your journey with your new family, for joining a new congregation is like joining a family. This family's members are just as much a part of your life as your own blood relatives. Perhaps they become even more a part of your life because we are all members of the same family, related through the Blood of Christ.

Think of this book, then, as an integral part of being welcomed to the fold, along with the friendly usher who warmly greets you by name, the older member who helps you navigate the service, and the hostess who makes sure you have a drink, a cookie, and someone to talk to as you shyly try to socialize with strangers during coffee hour. As you read its offerings, study the Scripture verses, sing the hymn lyrics, and pray the suggested prayers, may you find, at just the right times in your own spiritual journey, the words of encouragement and understanding that you need. They were written for and to you because we are not strangers but friends, family members who have yet to meet. With God's love and peace, and through the love that you are discovering within the church, may you know that you are not alone.

God bless! Welcome!

The Lord said to Abram, "Go from your country and your kindred . . . to the land that I will show you." So Abram went . . . to the land of Canaan.

(Genesis 12:1, 4–5)

Abram did not hesitate to answer God's call positively. He left Ur, went to Canaan, and ultimately began a multitude of nations. Like many other biblical characters after him, Abram willingly allowed himself to be in a new situation. He was called to a new place to accomplish God's blueprint for the world.

It may not be obvious to you why you decided to join your new parish, but a special place is held for you here as part of God's inimitable plan. Leaving one congregation and joining another is quite similar to Abram's leaving Ur. You have left your kindred spirits in one place and responded to the need to join others in a new one. And, like Abram, you had a choice to either respond to that need or to ignore it.

What would have happened if Abram hadn't said yes to the Lord? What if he had stayed in Ur? Historically, it was a large, important city in a flourishing civilization. Abram was deemed to be well educated and was probably a leader in the community. With all that anyone could want, why did he need to pack up his wife, nephew, and all of his possessions to move into the unknown, simply on what might be considered by others to be a whim? By biblical standards, seventy-five years old isn't so ancient, but to move with no idea where God was leading would be daunting at any age.

Yet, Abram chose to leave. Childless, he was promised that his descendants would become a great nation. Look what happened: Barren Sarah finally conceived, and eventually twelve tribes came into existence. The foundations of three major modern religious traditions were laid. All because one man responded to God's call.

God, too, has called you to this new place. You may not start a new religion or sire a multitude of nations, but there is a reason why God is showing you this new land. The Lord is making you a promise. If you follow where you're being led, God will take care of you. Just like he took care of Abram.

*They confessed they were strangers and foreigners . . . for people
who speak in this way make it clear that they are seeking
a homeland.*

(Hebrews 11:13b–14)

Each new member wonders, Why am I here, in this church? What aspects will fulfill my needs? What will make me stay?

While church shopping, we experience things that we both like and dislike. At one parish, the choir's excellent rendition of an anthem and the moving liturgical service inspire us to stay for coffee hour, when, seeking friendliness, we are totally ignored. At another church, the priest reads an aimless sermon, altos sing off-key, and kids scream during communion when we most long for silence. But at the service's end, we are overwhelmed by joyously friendly members welcoming us into their midst.

I remember the experience of a friend. The first Sunday she visited a potential congregation, she plopped herself, her husband, and their three children into a center pew and literally drew out a scorecard to rate the ushers, choir, sermon, and liturgy. During coffee hour, she deliberately sat quietly with her family in the darkest corner of the parish hall, waiting to be greeted. A half hour later, the rector finally came over, only to be grilled about the Sunday school curriculum and the vestry's stewardship policy. Seeking a spiritual homeland for her family, she knew exactly what she wanted in a church. The congregation she sought would satisfy every one of her needs. Sadly, no community can do that. When she realized this, my friend finally chose a congregation with an active Sunday school program. Which of your needs are most important to you? Do soul-inspiring sermons far outweigh being ignored during coffee hour? Do joyously friendly, welcoming members matter more than an out-of-tune choir and children being noisy during communion?

As a newcomer, look for what matters the most to you, realizing that just as a spouse cannot meet all of the needs of his or her partner, a church most likely will not excel in every aspect of your spiritual life. You've probably selected this church because it offers the things that matter most to you, not because it offers everything perfectly. As you continue in fellowship with the church, you might want to keep in mind the things that brought you here in the first place, the things that matter the most to you. Then you'll be more willing to let go of what is less important.

"Go out into the roads and lanes, and compel people to come in, so that my house may be filled."

(Luke 14:23b)

After a long illness that kept me homebound and unable to attend services, I rented a small farmhouse in the country, far from the congregation where I had been a member. Early on a crisp autumn Sunday morning, just after moving in, I began searching for a new church.

My car must have had a mind of its own because, without realizing it, I found myself driving on a lonely dirt lane. A small white chapel was tucked behind a grove of trees, across the road from its parking lot. Braking to let church members cross, I heard faint but familiar organ music. A parishioner walked up to my window, thanked me for stopping, and then asked if I would care to worship with them.

I do not know what compelled me to accept his gracious invitation, but I did. Sitting in the back pew of the small sanctuary, I noticed that the attendance was sparse. However, feeling spiritually uplifted by the inspiring sermon and music, I lingered after the service to meet the members. Later that week, I received a beautifully handwritten note from the welcoming committee explaining that although many local residents knew about and are often asked to attend the church, only a few had joined. The letter then asked if I would consider becoming a regular member of their tiny parish. I did and subsequently received from this church my recommendation for ordination.

Not all new visitors to church receive, as I did, personally engraved invitations to join. Invitations to join Christ's community, like the one sent by the home owner in Luke's Gospel to attend a feast, are often implied and always open. Like the countryside residents living near the small church, the relatives, neighbors, and friends asked to the dinner made excuses not to attend. The host instead beckoned "the crippled, the blind, and the lame" (Luke 14:21b) from lanes and streets and alleyways to dine with him.

Through Jesus Christ, God sends a standing invitation to us to partake of his kingdom's great feast. We are hailed from dirt roads, tree-lined boulevards, and dim back alleyways that some of us do call home. It does not matter where you are from. As a newcomer to church, you don't need an engraved invitation to join the feast. You are always welcome.

Do not neglect to show hospitality to strangers, for by doing that some have entertained angels without knowing it.

(Hebrews 13:2)

Joining a new church is like any other new venture in life. You face the same challenge of a new set of circumstances, perhaps with some level of trepidation, wondering how the changes will affect your life and your spiritual journey.

As a computer consultant, I am a newcomer, a stranger, to a different company just about every three to six months, facing the same kinds of circumstances that I did when first joining a congregation. Everyone was already established in their roles and responsibilities, and as a stranger in their midst, I was often not sure what to expect. But then there was the realization that not only was I a stranger to them, but the already "established" members were also strangers to me. The not-so-familiar faces were newcomers to my life, as I was a newcomer to theirs. These strangers can also be angels, as I have discovered.

I know I am not, by any means, one of the angels Paul writes about. But there are definitely angels in a new church family who often turn out to be key people who change our lives or who positively affect the course of our journey.

When meeting new people, I am shy and insecure; I struggle to be outgoing and friendly. When I first joined my present congregation, I often sat alone in a wooden pew, hoping to be invisible. But one Sunday during the passing of peace, I noticed that one of the older "strangers" was just as shy as I was, offering others only a slight nod or a weak handshake. Leaving my seat, I mustered up my consultant's courage, purposefully strode down the aisle, and warmly hugged her.

"Our Lord's peace be with you! Thanks for becoming a member of my new family!" It took a lot for me to be hospitable, but I found her vigorously hugging me back.

During coffee hour, she asked me about my profession. The educational coordinator for a large company, she instantly hired me to develop training materials. As we worked on the project together, we became close friends. Now we sit together in a middle pew, warmly greeting our family members, boldly and unabashedly passing on God's peace.

Paul's words ring true. Without knowing what would happen, as a newcomer I greeted a stranger and found an angel.

In the beginning was the Word, and the Word was with God, and the Word was God.

(*John 1:1*)

The spiritual journeys of many newcomers begin with Scripture. Perhaps a biblical passage or a story that you've recently read or heard has inspired you to return to or attend church for the first time. Perhaps you are here to learn more about how God's written word may apply to your life, or perhaps you simply have come here to learn the stories of Christianity.

The liturgies of all Christian denominations are based upon Scripture. Reading and studying it outside of services can help you discover and understand more about the written word. As you begin worshiping with your church, you might also read the Bible. By doing so, you will give its lessons a chance to form part of the solid foundation necessary for your spiritual growth. Richard Hooker, an Anglican theologian in the 1500s, once described Scripture as the basis of our liturgy and belief. He called it one leg of the "three-legged stool of Christianity," naming tradition and experience as the other two. By studying Scripture, learning our Christian heritage, and applying their lessons in our daily life, we become God's people of faith.

John implies here that each spiritual journey begins with the acceptance of God's truth found in his written word. As you participate in worship services, listen carefully to the Scripture lessons being read. You may want to reread them during the week, reflecting upon their meaning, learning how God spread his message by working in the lives of others and how his word, truth, and love also work to help you through your own daily struggles. You might wish to join one of the church's Bible study groups, as well as regularly read one of the many annotated versions of the Bible to help further your understanding.

"In the beginning was the Word . . ." also means that the "word" is *logos*, Greek for reason, knowledge, and understanding. Some Christians believe that *logos* is the Holy Spirit, the second person of the Holy Trinity. John also implies that the Spirit of Christ, God's love, is eternal and therefore existed long before incarnation into the life of Jesus. As you study Scripture, you will soon realize its wonderful message: God's truth is eternal, that he always has loved us, and that he always will.

Worship the Lord with gladness; come into his presence with singing . . . Enter his gates with thanksgiving, and his courts with praise. Give thanks to him, bless his name.

(Psalm 100:2, 4)

I joined my home parish, as new members often do, out of sheer joy of God's presence in my life.

Every Sunday in my congregation, before we take our pews, we write down our prayer petitions on a sheet of paper to be read aloud during the Prayers of the People. Lists of the sick and recovering, of victims of life's tragedies, of people dying and dead seem endless, while those of joy, thanksgiving, and answered prayer are sparse. As a new member, I thought this small congregation must not have much to joyfully give praise about unto the Lord! Grateful for many blessings, I began filling up the thanksgiving category with entries, including my pets Frankie and Clare, sunshine, being published, and enough daily bread, hoping other parishioners would do the same. Thanksgiving, apparently, is infectious: Each succeeding Sunday, more and more thanksgivings were offered. They now fill up an entire page.

Some newcomers are bursting to share their blessings, but may feel uncomfortable doing what Psalm 100 calls us to do. Liturgy and hymns are liberally splashed with joyous and grateful phrases: "Let us give thanks to the Lord our God" (BCP, 333; BAS, 193). "O worship the Lord in the beauty of holiness" (BCP, 45; CP, 385). "It is right to give him thanks and praise" (BCP, 361; BAS, 193). Even *eucharist* is ancient Greek for "thanksgiving." Often as congregations, however, we focus more upon our needs instead of upon our blessings.

Misery may love company, but joyfulness lasts longer. Joy can make any somber event a celebration. During communion and thanksgiving, we offer gratitude for Christ's death and celebrate the mystery of his presence in the bread and wine. The service is replete with praise, love, and joy for his resurrection. We even celebrate Eucharist during funerals because death is birth into eternal life.

As a new member, you may have many sorrows, but you may also have numerous delights. Some of us have great material riches and others don't have anything, but we all are abundantly wealthy together in God's love. As you begin your spiritual journey here, try entering his gates with thanksgiving, worshiping him with gladness. Pray about your sorrows, but openly share your joys as well.

Guided by the Spirit, Simeon came into the temple . . . and praised God, saying, "Master, now you are dismissing your servant in peace, according to your word; for my eyes have seen your salvation [the Savior]."

(Luke 2:27–30)

A righteous and devout man, Simeon awaited Israel's release from Rome's oppression. The Holy Spirit promised Simeon that he would not die until he had met the Messiah. Working in Jerusalem, praying in the temple, he sought the Messiah in everyone. The Holy Spirit guides the elderly Simeon to where a young couple is entering the temple to present their newborn son. The family is following Hebrew tradition which requires that the mother and her firstborn male be blessed forty days after birth. Simeon instantly recognizes Christ in the baby. Taking the infant in his arms, he realizes the Holy Spirit's promise is fulfilled. He accepts his Savior, knowing that, having seen God's salvation of Israel, he will die in peace.

The affirmation within the commitment of our Baptismal Covenant to "seek and serve Christ in all persons" (BCP, 305; BAS, 159) is reminiscent of Simeon's affirmation when he saw Christ in Jesus. Like Simeon, who was called to find Christ in one person, we are called to look for Christ in all people. In the ancient Jewish Rite of Purification, when a child was presented at the temple, the mother was immersed in water. She was blessed, and the child was dedicated to God, recognized by name, and introduced to the congregation. During the sacrament of baptism, based upon these ancient rites, we are sprinkled with water, named, and accepted into our new family. We are committed to share in Christ's divinity, finding and serving Christ in each other.

Luke 2:27–32 comprises the *Nunc dimittis* canticle used in both forms of Evening Prayer (BCP, 66, 120; BAS, 90). Based upon Scripture, canticles normally follow the daily readings. As you pray "The Song of Simeon," be reminded that as a new member, you are blessed and accepted by those welcoming you into the church, those who are committed to recognizing the living Christ in you. And you, as well, are called to find Christ in them, as well as in other new members.

Seeking and serving Christ in others, you and your new family will realize the fulfillment of the Holy Spirit's promise, together seeing God's salvation to live, and die, in peace.

"Who is my mother, and who are my brothers?" And pointing to his disciples, he said, "Here are my mother and my brothers! For whoever does the will of my Father in heaven is my brother and sister and mother."

(Matthew 12:48b–50)

Joining a new congregation is very much like joining a family. The spiritual ties binding you to your new church family may be stronger than the blood connections to your physical one.

Most newcomers have been searching for a spiritual home, but they are still surprised when their new church also becomes their extended family. An extended family is one that reaches into the larger community, gathering members together because of common interests, experiences, and needs, taking care of each other as though they were blood relatives. Readily welcoming new members, extended families share many facets of life together, just like many church families do.

The concept of family in Jesus' world was flexible. Common bonds brought and kept people together. Although it seems that Jesus was radically denying that Mary and his brothers were his kin, he was actually saying that his family also included his followers. In essence, they were an extension of his family because of God's love and the keeping of his commandments.

They reached out to others, helping in other areas of their lives in the same manner that blood-related family members do. They worked together, providing food for one other, as well as spiritual nourishment. They kept watch while Jesus prayed. John, an apostle, took care of Christ's mother after his death. Joseph of Arimathea provided a grave. Staying together as a family, they subsequently followed Paul, caring for each other long after Christ's resurrection.

As a newcomer to my present congregation, I had theology and spirituality in common with its parishioners. But, being single and estranged from my own blood relations, I quickly learned what "the family of Christ" really means. When I was ill the first two months of attendance, members brought hot soup and had my prescriptions filled. A fellow parishioner offered to care for Frankie, my cherished Basset hound, while I attended a conference. When my cousin died, his name was added to the prayer chain.

Today, when traditional nuclear families often break up, we need to be flexible about whom we consider our "brothers and sisters," allowing our church to become our extended family. It's not just religious ties that bind, but the sharing of God's love that makes a new congregation a home.

*And they cast lots for them, and the lot fell on Matthias; and he
was added to the eleven apostles.*

(Acts 1:26)

It wasn't just by chance that Matthias was chosen as an apostle. He
had publicly followed Christ for some time before he was nominated.
The original eleven were careful about who was selected to join in their
preaching and forgiving. Acts 6:3 says, "Select from among yourselves . . .
men of good standing," advising us to be discerning about those chosen
to minister.

Much can be learned from the apostles. Too often newcomers are nominated to serve in church capacities before they learn the church's organiza-
tion and needs, even before the community knows them. Some churches,
eager to put fresh, new workers into the field, ask newcomers to join highly
visible committees without waiting for them to be in good standing in the
congregation. Wishing to swell active ranks, regular members may not be
mindful of new members; nor do they always carefully consider if the new
members meet the church's ongoing needs, or even if the church is meeting
the needs of the newcomers. Sometimes established members forget that

new members may be hurting or in need of spiritual comfort, or just want some time to settle in. Newcomers may be seeking a place to lay burdens down, not pick up additional ones. Yet, eager to be accepted, sometimes we too readily say yes when asked to serve.

What are your needs? Are you homesick after transferring into the community? Are you looking for a church that resembles the one you left? Returning to Christ's fold, are you seeking renewal, spiritual stability, and religious guidance? What is your response to the cheerful alto who asks you to join choir without hearing you sing? Is joining multiple committees early in your membership really meeting your needs? Is it fulfilling the congregation's needs?

Like Matthias, we should first strive to become "members of good standing" before becoming leaders. Don't feel bad about taking time to explore the church you are joining. Let its members thoughtfully understand your spiritual needs. Just as the apostles took time to know Matthias, let this new church discern your talents. Give yourself space to learn about and feel comfortable in your new surroundings. Then, when lots are finally cast and you are asked to participate in a committee or group, it won't be by chance, but by responsible intention.

I once was lost, but now am found, was blind but now I see.
(The Hymnal 1982: Hymn 671; CP, 352)

Some new members are people returning to church after a long absence. During the hiatus, many of us were often literally lost, without direction, sightless to what we truly love until God's hand beckoned us to come home again.

Ten years passed between my father's funeral and the next time I entered a church. It was a span of great emptiness. My father died on the cusp of my teen years and adulthood. He had supported me in all my endeavors, helping me through failures and cheering me on to many successes. I had just graduated from college and was about to start my first job on the local newspaper when he left me completely lost, without his guidance and encouraging words. Attending Mass together had always been a special time for us. He instilled in me a love of the liturgy and a powerful love of Christ. But I was so blinded by my rage at God for letting my father die that I sought revenge by not going to church.

A decade after his death, as I was strolling downtown one morning to buy the Sunday paper, I felt compelled to walk through the narrow doors of the Episcopal cathedral just as the 10:00 A.M. service was about to start. I don't know why I was called to do what I did, but I hesitantly took a back pew as the choir began to boldly and lustily sing "Amazing Grace," Dad's—and now my—favorite hymn. As tears flooded with sad memories, I got up to leave. But as "now am found" was sung, a hand squeezed my shoulder in the same manner that Dad did when proving a point.

"Now that you're here, why don't you just stay and join us?" asked the elderly gentleman next to me. The same age Dad would have been, this man shared his hymnal and taught me how to use the prayer book. I stayed on through the service, sobbing, and then smiling when he offered me a pack of pocket tissues.

I returned Sunday after Sunday until, finally familiar with the liturgy, I felt completely comfortable. By sharing a pew and communion, I focused less on what I had lost and more on rediscovering my Dad's wondrous legacy of love. After years of being lost, I was found, and home again.

"Lord . . . I am not worthy to have you come under my roof;
. . . But only speak the word, and let my servant be healed."
(Luke 7:6)

Feelings of unworthiness crop up during spiritual journeys, especially in the early stages of church membership. A newcomer might feel that he or she doesn't know enough Scripture to teach Sunday school. Another doesn't feel dignified enough to bear the chalice as a eucharistic lay minister. There isn't one among us who doesn't feel unworthy at one time or another. Yet, there isn't one among us who is not worthy to receive God's healing love.

The Roman officer in Luke's Gospel did not mean he was "not good enough" when he said that he wasn't worthy. Sympathetic to Jews in Capernaum, he had built a synagogue. He was worthy to convert to Judaism and become a new member of Jesus' followers, but Roman law banned circumcision, which was required of all Jewish males. The centurion meant that he felt unworthy to receive Jesus who, by Jewish law, would have been defiled had he entered the Gentile's house. By coming to meet Jesus, his "Lord," the centurion showed great faith that Christ would heal his slave by words alone.

Feeling unworthy is part of our human nature. We err, we sin, and we feel unworthy. But even though we may not feel worthy, we are. We were worthy for Christ to come among us, and we are worthy to be new church members. Seeking Christ's healing words, you may have overcome feelings of unworthiness to come to church, unlike many people whose feelings of unworthiness prevent them from ever attending. However, church is, as the priest of my congregation once put it during one of his inspiring sermons, "a hospital for sinners; a first aid station for unworthy feelings."

During worship, we pray that we are worthy to receive God and Christ's healing words so that we are saved from our sins. Our relationship with God may be one of humility, but it is not one of "not being good enough." When you are ready to join church activities, remember that you are worthy to sing in the choir, to assist during Communion, and to teach Sunday school. As you begin anew your life as a Christian in this church, pray for forgiveness—not for being human, but for your human feelings of unworthiness.

You are always worthy to receive Christ into your life so that your soul shall be healed.

"Let the little children come to me; do not stop them; for it is to such as these that the kingdom of God belongs."

(Mark 10:14b)

Having drifted away from the church many years ago, a young mother could not answer her three-year-old daughter's questions about God. Wanting her little girl to have the spiritual foundation that she did not have, the mother took her to an Easter Evening service for the first time. As church lights were lowered, choir and clergy, carrying lighted candles, began processing down the aisle. All was quiet until the little girl began to loudly sing, "Happy birthday to you, happy birthday to you . . ."

Chuckling with the congregation, the priest stopped the procession and walked over to the embarrassed mother trying to silence her child. Rather than asking them to leave, he explained that the little girl was right. The candles were in celebration of Jesus Christ, whose birth and subsequent death and resurrection brought light into the world. The minister then blessed the child, invited her to Sunday school, and continued the procession.

As the mother later began learning Bible stories and prayers along with her daughter, she found answers not only to her child's questions but also to her own. She continued to attend church and study Scripture, building her missing foundation for spiritual awareness.

Many newcomers come to church because of their children. Parents may be unable to answer their youngsters' questions about God, or they may wish to begin their children's religious education at an early age. Perhaps you are looking for additional help and support in raising your children with the moral and ethical values found in church that seem to be lacking in other organizations. Acknowledging that while it may take a village to raise a child, you may be realizing that it also takes a whole congregation to help develop a young person's religious knowledge and spiritual awareness.

Encouraging parents to bring their children to him to be blessed, Jesus states that children are just as important as adults. God's kingdom, in fact, belongs to them, and to us newcomer adults who, with a child's innocence, also seek Christ. Finding answers for our children, we often find them for ourselves. Not only does attending church because of your children provide them with opportunities to eagerly learn and imitate the lessons of God's love in their lives, but it also may make you more aware of God's presence in your own.

Christ may dwell in your hearts through faith, as you are . . .
grounded in love . . . that surpasses knowledge, so that you may be
filled with all the fullness of God.

(Ephesians 3:17–19)

Many people today seek spiritual enlightenment, trying to replenish an empty void in their lives, in their very souls. We need to heal quickly in today's fast-paced culture, and we are offered many ways to instantly find meaning, including joining sects or cults. Some people totally commit themselves to work or an activity that promises instant, permanent satisfaction. How to be spiritually fulfilled is the topic of numerous self-help books and radio and television talk shows. They promise to fill our empty feelings with "quick-fix" alternatives to the solutions that take longer to find in a loving church community.

A young couple I know, realizing that something was missing in their active professional lives, began searching for a parish where they would feel spiritually aware. They wanted to be part of a community from their first Sunday of attendance; they wanted the void in their lives to be immediately filled. For two months, they went to a different church each week, not becoming an integral part of any one of them. Instead of their emptiness being filled with community love and spiritual sharing, it increased. When I finally suggested that they stay in one denomination long enough to really listen to the message, they stopped searching and began attending one church. Having grounded themselves in their selected congregation, they are now studying Scripture, gradually becoming spiritually fulfilled.

It's okay to want to fill a void quickly. But, as Paul writes, it takes time to be based in one community long enough for Christ to dwell in your heart and fill it with his love. As a new church member, you may be seeking what is missing in your own life. If you have not yet found spiritual fulfillment or if you do not yet feel part of this community, consider spending more time here, as this verse suggests, to become more grounded in the love of the congregation. This community may not have the quicker solutions offered outside the church, but drawing near on a regular basis to listen to God's message delivered in the lessons, the sermons, and the liturgy will soon help you find Christ dwelling in your heart. Your knowledge of him, which passes all understanding, will, in time, satisfy your every spiritual need.

"Where you go, I will go; . . . your people shall be my people, and your God my God."

(Ruth 1:16b)

When I hear Ruth's words during a wedding ceremony, I chuckle because, you see, Ruth is not declaring her faithfulness to a new spouse as is commonly thought, but to Naomi, her mother-in-law.

Naomi was a Hebrew from Judah who had moved to Moab to escape famine. Her two sons married Moab women, Ruth and Orpah. After her husband and sons died, Naomi decided to return to Judah, where Moabs were despised. When Orpah returned to her own mother, Ruth chose to leave Moab and accompany Naomi home. In spite of religious differences, Ruth remained faithful and loyal to Naomi. Because Ruth loved her mother-in-law, she followed her to a new, unfamiliar land, where she married Boaz and became not only the great-grandmother of King David but also a direct ancestor of Jesus Christ.

Ruth's steadfast declaration applies to many church newcomer situations. You may have just married into this congregation where your new spouse is a member. A company may have recently transferred you here.

Perhaps your parents have selected this church for your family to attend. Or, like a friend of mine, you have followed the minister from your former church because of his or her inspiring sermons. When I returned to church after my father died, one of the main reasons I joined a denomination other than the one in which I was raised was because a close friend was a member.

God often calls us to walk new paths in our spiritual journey to do his work in different places by asking us to lovingly and faithfully follow certain people. Sometimes, we are asked to follow because there is a special task in the building and maintaining of his kingdom that needs to be accomplished. Often, it is because he wishes to bring us, our families, and our friends closer to him. Regardless of the circumstances that caused you to follow someone and become a new member of this congregation, you are here for a reason greater than a job transfer or close friends. They were the instruments through which God asked you to join this community of Christ. Just as he asked Ruth through Naomi to follow into Israel, he has asked you into this new congregation to loyally and faithfully help promote his words and spread his love.

A prophet, Anna . . . of a great age . . . never left the temple but worshiped there with fasting and prayer night and day.

(Luke 2:36–37)

For what was Anna praying so long and hard? Her husband of only seven years? Prophetic insights? For the Messiah? She was there when Simeon saw salvation in Jesus. Finally recognizing him, she welcomed Christ into her life. The prophecies were fulfilled. Her prayers had been answered.

This passage reminds me of my mother, Ann, who was Anna's age when she died. She also was a widow who constantly prayed. Rarely attending church during the last few years of her life, Mom said the Rosary for hours, praying for everyone: family, friends, neighbors, me. When anything good happened, she'd say, "My prayers have been answered."

Prayer can be an integral part of your spiritual life, not only while attending your new church but also on a daily basis. New to the congregation, it may take you a while to acclimate to its social settings—its get-togethers, committee schedules, canons, customs, and traditions. It might also take you some time to learn about the prayer traditions, but it may be worth the effort. All the other activities in a parish are just accoutrements of its primary work: praying.

Congregations pray and worship in many different formats. We celebrate the Eucharist together on Sunday using psalms, scriptural readings, prayers, and various service forms found in our prayer book. The hymn lyrics we sing are also prayers. As a congregation, we give thanks and praise and then, blessed, refreshed, and renewed, we depart in peace, going out into the world to love and serve the Lord.

During the week, you can say morning and evening prayers. There are many other ways to pray that you may also find helpful. You might continuously repeat a brief prayer, quietly whisper short supplications, read The Great Litany, silently mull over Scripture, or pray one of this book's devotionals. You don't have to be as zealous as Anna or Ann, but do try to be intentional about focusing your mind upon Christ and keeping his Holy Spirit in your heart, so that your soul may communicate freely with God. It doesn't matter how you pray; God is always listening.

Because of him each of his messengers succeeds, and by his words all things hold together.

(Ecclesiastes 43:26)

God's words: white globs of glue holding the shards of our broken spirits together!

After my mother's funeral, I did not take the time to adequately sort through her possessions. Salvaging jewelry, family heirlooms, Dad's watch, and a few pieces of antique furniture, I gave the rest to relatives and charity. Among the items I brought home was an oblong gold-gilded china pickle dish upon which she used to serve delicacies during holiday family feasts. This treasured keepsake now has a place of honor on my hutch ledge, ready to serve my own tasty snacks to my friends.

The ledge is also my cat Clare's favorite perch. One day I heard a plaintive mew and a tinkling crash. My precious memory of Mother was scattered all over my kitchen floor, swatted into thirty-six sharp shards. It took two months and a pint of glue to put it back together. However, a chunk of china still missing and glued seams showing, the dish is upon my ledge once more. Back in service, it seems even stronger after its ordeal.

Like this dish, we are all broken in some way. Perhaps this is what has brought you to the church at this time in your life. Fragmented by hurt, grief, or a personal tragedy, you seek support and healing. You require time to pick up the pieces and glue yourself back together. As children, however, many of us learned to just ignore what is broken in our world. Some were taught to "get on with life," to be stoic and strong, not to inflict our problems upon others. But giving the people of our new church a chance to help may allow them to exercise an important aspect of their ministry. God works through everyone around us. When we let others help "glue us together," we allow God's participation in our lives.

If you've come to worship because you are hurting in some way, tactfully make it known that you are here to partake of Scripture's healing balm. Then, listen closely to the lessons, the gospel, the sermon, and what God says to you through others. God's words, the trusty glue that binds us all together in wholeness, will mend what is broken in your soul. Give yourself the necessary time to let the pieces set so that all things in your life will hold together again.

Stronger than before, you can then help others to mend.

But now we are . . . dead to that which held us captive, so that we are . . . in the new life of the Spirit.

(Romans 7:6)

Raised in a family that did not attend church, a friend of mine did not have any sense of spirituality in her life until she began attending services at the church closest to the farm that she and her husband run. Since joining the congregation, she has become a new person.

"I was lost when I moved here," she related. "I came from suburbia, where you waved to everyone when you walked your dog. It's very rural here. I hated not seeing anyone when I walked my dog. I was seeking fellowship, to feel more rooted in this community. So I joined the local church and attended each Sunday morning just to meet the neighbors that live across our fields."

The church members, she discovered, came from many different Christian denominations. Often led by lay people, the services are very nontraditional. After a few months of attendance, she was asked to lead a prayer service.

"I had a great 'Aha' about God, the great 'I Am.' I realized that I was truly part of this community and that Spirit was in the middle of my life and in the middle of the lives of those I was leading in prayer. I no longer feel lost or disconnected. I now have a sense of being part of God's neighborhood, the community of Christ. My whole life has changed since I joined. I am different now that Spirit is with me. I have become a kinder, more loving, gentler person. I even enjoy walking the dog."

Many new members have found that since coming to church their whole lives have changed. Maybe the changes are not as dramatic as my friend's, but attending church does help newcomers to become new people.

What does that mean in the church? When we give up old ways, we die to our old lives. By becoming new church members, we have died to a life outside the community of Christ. Moving into God's neighborhood, we are beginning a new life. In this sense, we are reborn. Our old lives may have been centered around other things, other people, but our new lives are now centered around God. And as God becomes the center of our lives, everything changes. Even ourselves.

"But you will receive power when the Holy Spirit has come upon you."

(Acts 1:8)

During Jesus' ministry, his disciples were often impatient with him, demanding that he make immediate changes to their situation. They wanted him, right then, to free Israel from Rome's yoke, not yet realizing that God has his own timetable. Right after Christ's crucifixion, his followers were disoriented, confused, befuddled. Their leader was gone, and Rome still ruled. They were not sure what to do or where to go next. Appearing ten days before his ascension, the risen Christ tells them that they must still wait patiently to be empowered by the Holy Spirit before they could clearly understand and preach Christ's message.

Disorientation, like that of the disciples, happens to even the most seasoned consultant. One of my more recent assignments was with a company whose complex covered two square miles. For the first two weeks, I got lost each morning looking for the building in which I worked. Once in it, I couldn't find my desk, without assistance, in the maze of two hundred cubicles. I felt helpless, powerless, and ill-prepared.

"I'm so disoriented!" I impatiently exclaimed to another consultant after two weeks. "When will anything feel familiar?"

"It'll happen only when you're ready," she replied, suggesting that I continue to ask for help until everything was familiar.

One day, still hopelessly lost and constantly asking how to get to where I thought I was going, I noticed another consultant struggling to find his cubicle. Suddenly, I was a company expert. Everything unfamiliar became commonplace. My confusion dispelled, I gave him directions and then confidently walked alone back to my own office.

Disorientation happens particularly to first-time churchgoers, to whom nothing seems familiar. Clergy, chalice bearer, choir attire, rituals, liturgy, and even language are alien. You feel like a bewildered, befuddled stranger in a strange land. You impatiently want everything to become familiar.

Allow yourself time to acclimate. If you can't find the parish hall, Sunday school, or even the bathroom, ask where they are. Eager to be familiar and secure in your new surroundings before you are ready, you might be too shy or feel silly seeking assistance. Ask anyway. By seeking their assistance, you give other church members an opportunity to minister to you. Keep asking until you're no longer disoriented but able to help others—a "company expert" yourself, assisting newer members.

"No one after lighting a lamp puts it under the bushel basket, but on the lampstand."

(Matthew 5:15–16)

Covered by a bushel, a lit lamp's flame either burns out or burns the basket.

Christ's words are a metaphor. As shining lights of his love in the world, we also reflect the light of our God-given individual talents. Using these talents in the service of the church is as much a part of stewardship as the money we give. A good steward not only gives financially but also joyously offers his or her time and talents.

New members often ask, Where do I belong, fit in? Where can I best serve? Part of the answer is found in discerning and sharing your talents and interests with other members. If you are thinking you don't have any talents, think again. We all have at least one shining ability that can be shared.

Do you like to gourmet cook? Join the fellowship committee or pitch in to prepare a church supper. Sing? Join the choir. More introverted? How about linking up with the prayer chain or a spiritual sharing group? If tinkering is your thing, volunteer for a church clean-up day. Like to write? Pen a newsletter article. In all the congregations I've known, there was at least one committee or interest group for just about every member. One parish filled its need for a part-time Christian education coordinator with a retired school administrator who had just joined the church. During a coffee hour, she indicated that she deeply missed working with teachers. Not hiding her lamp, she now lights up Sunday school instructors with inspiration.

Another church's stewardship committee annually conducts a talent treasure hunt, replacing the intimidating committee sign-up sheet with a page of suggested talents. Parish needs are matched to parishioner talents and abilities, and new groups are developed as needed to meet diversified interests. As members light their talent lamps, chancel drama actors, newsletter writers, kneeler needlepointers, and green-thumbed gardeners are discovered.

Supporting church functions is also a great talent: savoring church suppers, listening to the choir, attending parish musicals, smelling roses. It's also a gift simply to be present, enjoying the efforts of fellow members.

Be not only a newcomer but also be a new "bringer" of your gifts. When you feel comfortable enough to begin the process of letting them be known, uncover your talents and let them shine.

"Come unto me, all who labor and are heavy-laden, and I will give you rest."

(BCP, 131; BAS, 238)

Comfort and solace are found in may different ways in the church. These comforting words are often prayed during the evening service of Compline. They invite us to lay down our burdens in order to be refreshed and renewed in the presence of the Holy Spirit, here in the soul's resting place, the community of Christ.

Taken from Matthew's Gospel (11:28-30), this passage relates Jesus Christ's sermon about John the Baptist. Jesus, well acquainted with Hebrew Scripture, is quoting from The Wisdom of Sirach, a book in the Apocrypha. "Come to me, you who desire me, and eat your fill of my fruits" (24:19) is from Sirach's poem about Wisdom, or Sophia, the feminine attribute of God in Judaic tradition, believed by some to be the Holy Spirit. Sirach reflects that God's wisdom in creation, in the tradition of Israel's covenants and Mosaic law, is present and available to Jews in the temple. By citing the poem, Jesus proclaims himself the spokesperson for Wisdom, inviting his followers to freely partake of Sophia's feast—her fruits and offerings of refreshment—to find rest, meaning, and purpose in daily life.

As a newcomer, you may be joining or rejoining the church because you need refreshment in some way. You may be wearily seeking relief from life's daily burdens, which may include sin, excessive work demands, various forms of abuse, oppression, depression, or even fatigue from searching for spiritual meaning. Some of you are ill, penniless, or even homeless. Praying these words in the midst of your strife and turmoil can bring comfort. The fruits of the Holy Spirit refresh, like cold citrus on a hot day!

The Holy Spirit is present and available to you in your new church home, where refreshment from the secular world is readily found. Sin is forgiven by her power. The Holy Spirit keeps you in eternal life. Wisdom can be found in liturgy and Scripture, reinvigorating what may have seemed meaningless, infusing it with spiritual renewal, productivity, and purpose.

What needs refreshing in your life? From what does your soul need rest? Joining a church may not instantly change your troubles, nor will it make them disappear. But freely partaking of the fruits of the Holy Spirit through liturgical prayer might help refresh and renew your attitude toward your cares, making them easier to bear.

The gifts he gave were that some would be apostles, some prophets, some evangelists, some pastors and teachers, to the saints for the work of ministry.

(Ephesians 4:11–12)

In the beginning of his ministry, Jesus selected his twelve apostles from different vocations. As Jesus walked the countryside, he called to his new apostles, "Follow me and I will make you fish for people" (Mark 1:17). While the pun "fishers of men" in the King James Version of the Gospels is more amusing than the wording used here, Jesus' saying affirms in any translation that his apostles and disciples were from all walks of life. Paul tells us in his letter to the Ephesians that each one also had unique spiritual gifts to share in serving Christ. Compelled to unquestioningly follow Jesus, the apostles offered these gifts to serve in different capacities to become his ministers, spreading his word of God's love and peace.

Like the apostles, you have been equipped with unique spiritual gifts by the Holy Spirit to be a minister within the church. This does not mean that you have to be ordained to serve. Through baptism, you are automatically assigned the same tasks as the apostles: preaching and spreading God's truth and love. *Ministry* means "attending to the needs of others." Everything Christians do, in and out of the church, is a ministry. So, as a new member, you too are a minister, discovering and sharing your spiritual gifts, serving as one of Christ's followers.

There are many ways to be a minister, living your faith both outside the church, in your work and home life, as well as within. If you are uncertain about how best to serve, there are a number of paths within the church to follow in discovering your spiritual gifts and what your ministry might be. You might seek clergy guidance in beginning your journey of discovery, or you may decide to join a study group, like Education for Ministry, that is specifically geared to aid lay church members in determining how they can best learn about and use their spiritual gifts to attend to the needs of others.

As you discern your new vocation, remember that you are closely following Jesus in the footsteps of his twelve apostles. However you decide to use your gifts, you are always a minister of Christ.

*As the people were filled with expectation, and all were questioning
in their hearts concerning John, whether he might be the Messiah . . .*
(Luke 3:15)

John the Baptist's followers were full of questions about him. They asked
why he called himself "the voice of one crying out in the wilderness," telling
them to "Prepare the way of the Lord" (Luke 3:4). Was he their long-awaited
Messiah? When John said, "One who is more powerful than I is coming"
(3:16), the people realized that he was not what they expected him to be.
Often, congregations anticipate that new members have the same social
status, ethical views, and theological beliefs as their longtime members.
More often than not, like John, newcomers to a church are not always what
is expected.

Last year, a single mother of two joined a congregation that was
recommended by a neighbor. When she was told that she would be expected
to participate in the women's social fund-raising group, she began questioning
the church's expectations for new members. Struggling to hold down a
full-time job and needing to devote her free time to raising her children, she
discovered that the congregation's social activities, primarily geared for

two-parent families, were not in keeping with her own lifestyle. However, because the church's theology and worship services were in line with her own beliefs, she still decided to become a member. She soon met other members who were also without life partners. They, too, were feeling left out of many of the church's activities. Within months she did the unexpected and started a group for the church geared to meeting the needs of its single members.

As a newcomer, you are expected to regularly attend services, adhere to an outline of faith, and be a good steward of your time, talents, and treasures. But you might also be expected to flow with the established mainstream and, like the single mother, to participate in activities that conflict with your own lifestyle.

Openly inquire about this parish's social functions and values. If you don't agree with them, don't change your perspectives or lifestyle just because you feel it is expected of you. Like John the Baptist, whose words and actions were not what the crowd was looking for, you may not be what the church anticipated. But with your own different perspectives, like John, you might be pointing the way to questioning and changing current expectations, helping to develop new ones that will benefit the church.

O come, all ye faithful, joyful and triumphant.
            (The Hymnal 1982: Hymn 83; CP, 118)

One of the most popular Christmas carols, this hymn universally calls all who are "faithful" to "adore him, Christ the Lord." Blared from radio and television during the Yuletide season, the song provides sentimental reasons for lapsed Christians to flock back to church and for new seekers of spiritual truth to enter for the first time. In many churches, attendance soars during the holidays, with sanctuaries swelling to "standing room only" capacity during Christmas Eve services.

If as a newcomer you've chosen to attend church during the celebration of Christ's birth and have subsequently decided to join, you know that worshiping with a congregation is more than just the festivities of Christmas. Christmas is undoubtedly the season to share in God's triumph with the birth of his only Son and to express our joy in Christ's arrival. This verse, however, really says that our joy is continuous. It lasts not just during the holidays, all aglow with candlelight, liturgical richness, and stirring music, but forever, because Christ is born to eternally triumph for us sinners over darkness, evil, and sin.

Attending church for the first time or as a returnee is a major life decision. It ranks right up there with deciding whether to be single or coupled, electing to raise children, and choosing where to live and work. Deciding where to worship may affect not only this life but also the next. Your decision is not one to be taken lightly. Each time you come to worship in church, you are part of the "faithful."

You may have been filled with glad tidings during Christmas, but your choice to continue attending church on a regular basis to adore him as a truly faithful member is joyously triumphant. Long after Christmas lights and sparkling tinsel have faded into Lent's darkness, you will still be singing with this church "in exultation . . . embracing him with love and awe."

"I am the light of the world. Whoever follows me will never walk in darkness but will have the light of life."

(John 8:12b)

I left the church out of revenge for my father's death. My mother's passing scared me back, slamming home the realization of my own mortality. I was now no longer Ann's child, but an adult heading toward old age and eventual demise. Frightened by my mother's death and the contemplation of my own, I came back to church after another absence that lasted two years, seeking comfort and consolation.

In a sermon I once heard, the priest said, "Facing death can be a scary prospect. It can also be a miraculous anticipation. It is the continuation of our spiritual journey with Christ, the next great adventure. All we have to do is walk in his light." Thinking about these words and those of John, I began to be solaced. Above anything else, Christ promises us eternal life. This is why he was born, to conquer death for us. Belief in the promise of life after death is a primary reason we come to church. We come together to pray and to prepare our souls for death and our entrance into eternal life.

Death of a loved one sometimes brings people back to church or into church for the first time. In deep sorrow and reminded of their own mortality, most mourning newcomers—sometimes angry, often questioning—want answers, sympathy, and relief from grief. If you're here because someone close to you has died, this is the most appropriate place and time to begin your spiritual journey. You are walking out of darkness to follow the "great light" of Christ, God's promise of eternal life.

The fundamental basis of Christianity, Christ's promise of eternal life, was prophesied in the Old Testament by Isaiah: "The people who walked in darkness have seen a great light; . . . on them light has shined" (9:2). It is this light, another meaning of *logos*, that John says exists from "the beginning . . . the light of all people," the light of the Holy Spirit, the light of Christ that "shines in the darkness, and the darkness did not overcome it" (John 1:1–5). Walking into church to follow Christ's light of life rekindles the light in our souls. Never overshadowed by the darkness of sin and death, God's presence comforts and consoles, promises salvation, and guides us always in our journey onward into eternity.

"Give therefore to the emperor the things that are the emperor's, and to God the things that are God's."

(Matthew 22:21; Mark 12:17)

At some point in your new church membership, you are asked to fill out a pledge card. While we may be seeking refuge from a materialistic world and prefer not to deal with money matters at church, tending to the financial stewardship of our spiritual families is also part of becoming a faithful servant. If you are brand new to worshiping in a church, you may be apprehensive about being asked for financial support. You may have heard others complain about denominations that "only care about money." Although economics may sometimes seem to be their only focus, the majority of congregations simply need to meet ever-increasing operational costs. Churches cannot run their physical plants without regular contributions that are freely given from the congregation.

Quite understandably, being solicited for pledges immediately upon joining a parish may turn off new members. It might help to think of your new congregation as a family with a yearly budget. Just as you know your own household's yearly income, church administrators need to have an idea of how much money they will have to work with over the coming year, in order to be able to properly budget to meet expenses. The church, too, as a family, needs to pay the bills necessary to continue its very existence.

In both accounts of Jesus' response to the Pharisees' questioning, he shows that we owe citizens' allegiance both to our state government and to God's kingdom. As state members, we are required to pay for the goods and services we receive, as well as to pay our taxes. As citizens of the kingdom of heaven, we are primarily pledged to obey and commit ourselves to God. Good stewardship means that we return a portion of the money, time, and talents that God has entrusted to us, gladly giving back to God what is his.

As a newcomer, the pledging of a portion of your income to your new church is an outward and visible sign that you accept and commit to being here, where you truly belong. Abraham, who pledged ten percent of his worldly goods to the temple priest Melchizedek, set the standard for tithing. However, realizing that not everyone can afford to tithe, many church leaders suggest that you offer what you can at present and then try to gradually increase your contribution over time. Whatever you do pledge, give it faithfully and joyously. You are helping your congregational family meet its economic obligations so that it can focus upon the spiritual needs of its members and the spreading of God's love.

"It is easier for a camel to go through the eye of a needle than for someone who is rich to enter the kingdom of God."

(Matthew 19:24)

This saying of Jesus deeply concerned a friend of mine when he first joined a suburban church. At the time, he was enjoying a very profitable business career. Not quite understanding the parable's full meaning, he took the words literally and to heart. The more money he made, the less and less confident he became that he would eventually be able to enter God's house. An affluent newcomer hearing these words, he was reluctant to fully participate in church activities, feeling as he did that it would be almost impossible for him, a wealthy member, to gain admittance into God's kingdom.

This passage has many interpretations, and its meaning is often debated. In the time of Christ, the Eye of the Camel was one of Jerusalem's gates through which only camels and the poor were allowed. Hence, a rich person would be denied access to the city through this gate and would have to find another entrance into Jerusalem. In this analogy, a rich person would also be denied access to heaven unless he became poor enough to follow the way of Jesus into heaven's gate.

Camel is also a Hebrew word meaning "a bit of coarse yarn," which can be softened and woven into fine cashmere only after a lot of hard work. In this second analogy, a person with great wealth may find it difficult to put aside amassing worldly possessions. However, it is still possible, with hard work and sacrifice, for someone to reweave what is most important in his or her life and to forego attaining riches in order to follow the teachings of Christ.

But what Jesus is actually reminding us of here is the second commandment, "You shall have no other gods before me." Those of us blessed with material riches should not put the accumulation and enjoyment of our wealth above or before our love of God. Yet, some affluent new church members refrain from fully committing to and participating in the work of Christ's community because it may not seem rewarding or profitable. In truth, it might prove to be their most prosperous activity. To ensure our eternal reward, all we need do is place God before, and into, our worldly endeavors.

As my friend has since learned, God is not so much concerned with how well-to-do we are, but with how well we do with the wealth he has given us.

Blessed is he who comes in the name of the Lord.

(BCP, 373; BAS, 193)

Islamic tradition ascribes ninety-nine different names, or attributes, to God. The reason for this is that they believe that God is everywhere. By memorizing and reciting these ninety-nine names, through an act known as *dhikr* in Arabic, Muslims can look at the world and witness the divine in everything and every situation. As a newcomer, this is a wonderful way for you to realize that there is an attribute or aspect of God that can help with whatever situation that caused you to come to church for the first time or to return after being away for a long time.

Did you come for solace? God is The Compassionate. For forgiveness? God is The Pardoner. God is also The Forgiving, The Provider, The Creator, The Merciful, The Truth, and The Light, just to name a few. In fact, God has about three thousand names if you add up all those mentioned in the Torah, the Arabic Zabur book of Psalms, the New Testament, and the Koran. All these aliases of our one God attest that there is no place that God isn't. "There is not a spot where God is not."

You have newly come to church for a reason. Something or someone has caused you to seek, to search, to share your spiritual quest with this congregation. As a new member, it is sometimes difficult to realize that you are blessed just because you came to church. *Blessed*, meaning "fortunate," also means "seeking God's divine favor." In such searching, our lives are automatically, without reservation, consecrated, sanctified, and made holy with the divine presence. Regardless of why you are here, you have come in God's name, in whatever name you wish to use to call him or her. Simply because of that, God is present in your life. You are blessed.

As a new member, note that God may be addressed in many ways. In an effort to make the church more "politically correct," some call God "her" or have eliminated gender-specific references from the liturgy. Some members, stating that God has the attributes of both genders, use the pronoun "El," as in "God spoke to all of El's people." It doesn't matter to God what we call him, her, or El. What does matter is that as new members, we've come to call. And that by doing so, in all of God's names, we are truly blessed.

If anyone is in Christ, there is a new creation: everything old has passed away; see, everything has become new! All this from God, who . . . has given us the ministry of reconciliation.

(2 Corinthians 5:17–18)

Divorce, moving far from home, the loss of a loved one—all of these can be painful. During the period of readjustment, one can feel estranged and isolated from human relationships. Divorced or separated newcomers sometimes feel lonely, embarrassed, or rejected. New residents of a strange town may feel lonely. Those in mourning are often disoriented, questioning their deep loss. With no place else to turn, they may come to church seeking a sense of community, companionship, and meaning. Perhaps, after a major rupture in your life, you have come to find comfort, consolation, and renewal within God's community. Isn't this the most important reason why you are here?

With your life split asunder, you can look to the church as the place where you can again belong, feel accepted, and begin your life anew. Regardless of how lost, disoriented, or discouraged you might feel, you are always welcomed by and reconciled to God. Paul implies that even if you do have irreconcilable differences with a former spouse, feel that nothing is familiar in your new surroundings, or are uncomfortable being without your loved one who has died, you shouldn't be discouraged. We are assured by this passage that anyone who comes to Christ finds "a new creation."

Through the Holy Spirit, you have a new beginning in this congregation. Regardless of the reasons for your divorce, loneliness, or sadness, you will find that the established members of your new church community are welcoming, wishing to help you heal your pain, providing companionship and comfort through their unconditional fellowship. Through these welcoming members, there is your promise of renewal and reconciliation with Christ. Through them, you can develop new life-affirming relationships and find comfort and consolation in your new church home. No longer feeling isolated and lonely, you will quickly find that you belong here in the loving, reconciling community of Christ.

. . . and giving voice to every creature under heaven, we acclaim you and glorify your Name.

(BCP, 373; BAS, 207)

When I first joined my present congregation, the priest asked what I held most dear in my life. He smiled when I told him about the joy and unconditional love my companion pets, Frankie and Clare, bring to me and to those they sometimes visit in nursing homes and children's hospital wards.

"Then pray with and for your animals," he said. "When we pray, we pray with and for everyone, every being in our life. Our prayers speak to God with and for every other creature God has made. Prayer is the giving of thanks and praise for each and every minute aspect of creation." This was a startling revelation to me. I had not considered that by coming to church I was bringing with me in spirit, as well as in thought, everyone and everything else in my life, including my cherished hound and beloved cat. God's love, the priest explained, extends over all his universal creation, not just to human beings.

Although some don't believe animals and plants have souls, I have come to believe that God's Spirit is manifested in all of his creation. According to

Paul in his letter to the Colossians, when the good news of Christ was spread, it was "proclaimed to every creature under heaven" (1:23). Because it is not only our own voices in our prayers, but other voices as well, I began a new family custom. Several nights a week, all my household members, including pets, gather for Evening Prayer. It is read out loud so that even the animals hear our voices acclaiming and glorifying God's holy name.

When attending church for the first few times, most newcomers feel that they are going for themselves. You may sit alone in what seems like an empty pew, but it is filled with those you've brought with you in your heart. You are there not only for yourself but also as the representative of others that are part of your daily life. While they may not be physically in attendance, your friends, relatives, neighbors, coworkers, and yes, even your pets are symbolically there with you. By keeping them in your thoughts and prayers, you are giving them a voice through which they, too, can give thanks and praise to God for their creation.

Be still, and know that I am God.

(Psalm 46:10)

When some of us are still and quietly listening, we may hear a little voice inside us that we believe is God's calm and soothing presence.

A newcomer joined a church because of its serenity. He felt it each time he entered the peaceful sanctuary where, in the midst of the turmoil of his daily life, he could quietly be in God's presence. Now when pressures at work and home begin to mount up during the week, he takes time to quietly remember praying in the sanctuary. By being still, the new member senses and is calmed and renewed by God. These brief moments of prayer make it easier for him to cope with the hectic demands of his busy life.

Psalm 46 was written when the known world was beset with threats of war and destruction. The writer realized that in the midst of the most frightening turmoil, God was always with his people. Back then, when besieged and stressed out by problems, God's followers took the time to be still, to quietly pray for peace and guidance. In their still thoughts and prayers, they renewed their confidence that God would take care of them.

It can be difficult in today's busy world to take a moment to be still and acknowledge God. This is especially hard when so many of us have hectic schedules and are feeling overwhelmed. Yet, taking an occasional minute in the midst of the commotion and hubbub of our daily lives to entertain God's presence is not so different from counting to ten or imagining that we are in a quiet, safe place. Instead of counting or imagining, spend a moment with God. With a brief, silent prayer, call upon God's peace and understanding to be with you to respond, not react, to urgencies. Praying for help and assurance, we know that God is eternally our storm's calm center.

As a new member, you have joyously opened the door of the church's still, peaceful surroundings to find inner serenity. What you are feeling when you worship here is the peace of God: the still, quiet voice that you can hear whenever you wish, wherever you are. A brief moment in prayer, anytime, anywhere, affirms that God is, indeed, in every aspect of our lives.

Every day he was teaching in the temple. . . and all the people would get up early in the morning to listen to him.

(Luke 21:37–38)

Imagine that it is two thousand years ago. Dawn is breaking over Jerusalem's east gate. Someone pounds on your door, awakening you from a deep sleep. He excitedly shouts, "Jesus of Nazareth is teaching in the temple!" Curious about whether this is the Savior come at last, you hasten out of your stone home into the already sweltering day, joining the throng on its way to hear the one who claims to be the Messiah.

Back then, as they do now, people clamored for God's assurances. Seeking miracles that would prove God's existence, they followed any charlatan alleging to be their savior. When the imposter's miracles and promises proved false and empty, the crowd quickly dispersed to seek their messiah elsewhere.

During the week before Jesus was arrested and crucified, the people of Jerusalem had a wonderful opportunity. They could begin each day listening to his authentic message. Imagine your excitement as you become one of the first to receive God's promise of peace, love, and eternal life.

Believing that, unlike false prophets before him, Jesus was the only true Savior, you would have wanted to share your joy.

The people in the temple began sharing Jesus' words with others that were not his followers. Many decided to follow Jesus, becoming new members of his circle of friends, just as you have recently chosen to become a new member of this church. Sharing God's wondrous message with families, friends, and acquaintances, the new members of Jesus' entourage spread God's word throughout the known world and throughout the ages.

Having newly joined this church, you have the same opportunity as the new disciples of Jesus. Each morning and evening when you attend a worship service, you are hearing the same message that Jesus delivered in Jerusalem's temple. Just about everything else has changed from what it was in Christ's time, but the word of God has not. It is just as applicable to life today as it was back then. You don't have to imagine delivering the message of true salvation to others twenty centuries ago. You are doing today exactly the same thing the new members of the early church did: joyously sharing God's message of eternal peace and love.

He said to her, "Daughter, your faith has made you well; go in peace, and be healed of your disease."

(Mark 5:34)

A dear friend of mine, deeply hurt and betrayed by her husband, who had been unfaithful for the last half of their ten-year marriage, finally decided to end it. Uncertain about how to begin the process of healing, she thought that going to church might provide her with the comfort and support she needed. Since she hadn't been to services since her wedding, she began asking friends about the churches they attended. One acquaintance suggested a large congregation whose pastor was also a psychologist. Feeling ashamed and afraid of being rebuked for seeking divorce, my friend postponed attending services and calling the minister for counseling until one particularly restless Saturday night.

Normally a sound sleeper, she was suddenly awakened at 3:00 A.M. with a compelling desire to go to church. Ignoring the compulsion, she drifted back to sleep only to be awakened again at 5:00 A.M. with the same feeling. Unable to go back to sleep, she waited until 8:00 A.M. to call the church's office for directions and service times. During worship that morning, she began to feel solaced and afterward scheduled counseling sessions with the pastor. To her relief and surprise, he was not reprimanding but consoling. He explained that because of her faith in seeking guidance, she would be quickly healed of her feelings of guilt and betrayal. Within months, my friend felt well enough to complete the divorce proceedings and begin her new life as an active member of the church.

Often, newcomers are afraid to ask clergy for counseling. If you are a new member in need of guidance from a minister, do not be reluctant to request help. Clergy are Christ's representatives here on earth. By seeking an ordained minister's help in times of trouble, we are symbolically touching Jesus' robe. Consider the woman who feared Jesus' rebuke for touching his robe, but did so anyway and was healed. Consider my dear friend who feared being reprimanded for divorcing her husband but followed her compelling feelings to attend a church, where she found spiritual guidance and the help she needed to get on with her life. Because they faithfully believed they would be healed, they "reached out to touch" and became whole again, just as you can too.

I sing a song of the saints of God . . . and I mean to be one too.
                                    (*The Hymnal 1982: Hymn 293*)

The denomination in which I was raised painted a grim picture of what it took to be a saint. As a child, my perception was that in order to be one, you had to wear sackcloth, be covered in ashes, and perform miracles. If living a hard life wasn't enough, you also had to be martyred for Christ, dying a grisly death by being eaten by lions, pierced by arrows, stabbed with a sword, or burned at the stake. The standards were frighteningly high for a seven-year-old. I knew I would not be able to meet them, yet not doing so meant missing being in heaven with Jesus.

When I grew up and began attending services of another denomination, I began to sing these bright and cheering lyrics by Lesbia Scott. She wrote them so that her young daughter would understand that all those who willingly come to God are saints.

The word *saint* originated from *sanctus*, Latin for "holy" and "consecrate." In most Christian denominations, a saint is simply anyone who is a member, living or dead, of the church and who is devoted to knowing and serving God. Saints come from every walk of life and are found everywhere. As the second verse says, they loved "their Lord so dear . . . they followed the right, for Jesus' sake." For me as a newcomer, this was an inspiring concept. It encouraged me to stay and join my new church. I didn't have to wear rags, eat locust, or perform wondrous miracles. Best of all, I didn't have to die first to become a saint. As a newcomer of the congregation, joining in the celebration, I already was one.

Becoming a new member, I found myself in the company of all kinds of saints. Not only did I meet those listed in Scott's verses, but I also met attorneys, veterinarians, chefs, mechanics, plumbers, roofers, painters, artists, secretaries, writers, and even politicians. I met hungry, homeless, impoverished, illiterate, diseased, incapacitated, and disabled saints. I met elderly ones, as well as young and innocent ones. And as a new member, I felt quite at home, as you will too, in the company of all these saints, who are folks just like you and me who joyously brighten up the world with their love of doing Jesus' will.

. . . so that you have genuine mutual love, love one another from the heart.

(1 Peter 1:22)

When you first meet some people, don't they seem familiar to you? It's almost as if they were already your friends.

The next time you go to church, take a closer look at members of the congregation. Even though you are a new member and haven't yet met everyone, don't many of them seem familiar? Almost as if you've met the lady in the yellow dress or the young usher or the elderly couple in the front pew somewhere else before, but you just can't quite place where or when.

The first letter of Peter was written to church members in the Roman provinces of Asia Minor when Christianity was still a new religion. The writer earnestly urges his readers to have hope and faith at a time when the church and its new system of ethics were despised. Roman officials persecuted church members so that their novel religion wouldn't corrupt society's existing morals and political structure. Converts to the early church were newcomers like yourself, called to spiritual rebirth and renewal through God's word and works. Peter suggested to these new church members that they warmly welcome and love each other as friends, even though they might be strangers, whenever they gathered to pray and break bread together. In welcoming other new members, each one was to express genuine mutual love from the heart, as they sought friendship among themselves.

A usher/greeter in a congregation in Philadelphia (the Greek word for "genuine mutual love") greets each newcomer by saying, "Welcome, friend. It's good to finally meet you." His philosophy is in keeping with Peter's: that strangers are friends that he hasn't yet met. The church, he says, is the one welcoming place where "strangers meet friends who meet strangers," where God's unconditional love is to be unreservedly shared with newcomers. The church accepts us and loves us as friends, regardless of who we are, what we do, and where we are from.

New to this church, you are hopefully finding it to be a welcoming place. Even though at first its members may seem like strangers to you in the secular sense, they are all your spiritual friends in Christ.

Perhaps that is why they seem so familiar.

"If you ask anything of the Father in my name, he will give it to you. . . . Ask and you will receive, so that your joy may be complete."
(John 16:23b–24)

In the past, Jewish believers prayed to God through temple priests who approached God on the people's behalf. In John's Gospel, however, Jesus says that when one begins a new relationship with God, there is no need for anyone else to intercede. Anyone can approach God for and by themselves, talking with him on a personal level, just like chatting with a friend or a member of the family. Those who ask God directly for what they want will be directly answered.

There's an old joke about a little boy who, after giving a wrong answer on a geography test in school one day, asked God during his prayers that night to "please make Toledo the capital of France." Although a joke, it reminds us of the truth. We can personally ask God for anything, at anytime. Through his own son, Jesus Christ, God has promised that whatever we ask for will be received. God probably won't change the name of a city just so we can pass a test, but he can and will do other things in our lives. All we have to do is ask.

In an episode of a popular television show, an angel asked a couple about to be married if they had invited God to the wedding ceremony. The angel explained to the bride and groom that their journey together wouldn't work until they had fully welcomed God's love into their lives. All they had to do was ask.

When you decided to become a member of this church, you committed yourself, like newlyweds do, to a new relationship in which God is the central reason for the alliance. He is always available to hear your prayers to directly to help you as you begin your spiritual journey with your new congregation.

Welcome God's love fully into your life, so that as you continue to pray with this church's clergy, lay ministers, and members, he will eternally be there to help and guide you. By personally inviting God into your life, to be with you always, you know that you will receive whatever you need. As Jesus promised, all you have to do is ask.

The Lord your God . . . will exult over you with loud singing.
(Zephaniah 3:17)

Now that you've begun or restarted your spiritual journey within this church community, consider that you and its members are not the only ones rejoicing. While you are praising and glorifying God during worship services, he, in turn, is rejoicing over your being here.

Imagine God joyfully singing, as he does in this quote from Zephaniah. In the last passage of this short book from the Old Testament, the prophet calls for the people of Israel to exultantly shout and sing. The young king Josiah has spurned their enemies and has set in motion reforms that will restore the Hebrew religion to the land. The people are invited to publicly renew their spirituality. When they do, God will rejoice with them and sing over them. In his writings, Zephaniah reminds us that we too, just like the Israelites in his time, are often in need of spiritual renewal and restoration. If this is the reason you are in church, God is greatly rejoicing over the fact that you have come to him in your quest.

Three of Jesus' parables parallel Zephaniah's message. Although their plots are not alike, "The Lost Sheep," "The Lost Coin," and "The Prodigal Son and His Brother" (Luke 15: 1–32) all relate the same great elation in finding someone or something very precious that had been lost. A shepherd leaves his whole flock alone in the wilderness to seek the one sheep that strayed and was missing. Finding it, he calls his friends and neighbors to join him in rejoicing. A father invites the neighborhood to a feast of celebration when his wayward son returns. A woman calls all her friends and neighbors to come celebrate with her when, after lighting a lamp and cleaning her whole house, she finds the lost one of her ten gold coins. These stories are different examples Jesus used to explain that God celebrates each and every time someone finds his or her own unique way into the community of Christ.

Both the parables and Zephaniah's words affirm that God rejoices in response to our becoming new members of his fold. We are all indeed precious to God, and now that we are here in his church, imagine him rejoicing over us. Picture him eternally celebrating, singing his joy as we sing his praises.

"I am the true vine, and my Father is the vinegrower. He removes every branch in me that bears no fruit. Every branch that bears fruit he prunes to make it bear more fruit."

(John 15:1–3)

Gardeners know that cutting away dead limbs and new growth promotes more fruitful blooms. It isn't enough that I planted my rose bushes in the backyard to catch the morning sun. I have to remember to water them regularly and to properly nourish and deeply mulch them at the appropriate times. No matter how hard I try, I can't seem to keep up with the dead branches that refuse to produce blossoms. Sadly, I have to diligently cut away the lifeless limbs and then carefully prune the live branches so that each bush continues to produce an abundance of hardy roses.

As a new member, think of yourself as a new sprout on the vine of the congregation. When a new branch appears, a commitment is made between it and the plant. The plant provides water and nourishment from the soil in which it is growing; the shoot partakes of the water and nourishment to bring forth abundant fruit. God, the gardener, has a covenant with you, the new limb, and his church, the plant, to mulch the soil and to prune the branches. It is up to you, as a new sprout on this congregation's bush, to make proper use of its nourishment from the good soil of its loving fellowship. In doing so, you will be able to produce good fruit.

Some branches on the church's vine make the superficial commitment to join a worshiping community and then refuse to partake of the nourishment that is offered. They eventually fall away and leave the garden. Those branches that partake of the nourishment offered are believers who fully commit to a union with Christ. These new sprouts, like yourself, blossom into established members. They produce good fruit, living out their faith not only within the church but also outside its sanctuary walls in all aspects of their lives.

As a new member, may the Holy Spirit, through Scripture, water you. May Christ's basking sun, shining through other members of the congregation, nourish you. May you be fruitful and grow, producing great and glorious blossoms.

"So then, you are no longer strangers and aliens, but you are citizens with the saints and also members of the household of God . . ."
(Ephesians 2:19)

In Luke's passage about the Roman centurion, Gentiles could not join Jewish communities. But in his letter to Gentiles in Ephesus, Paul explains that those separated from the new Jewish sect could now join them in worship because Jesus' death and resurrection had "abolished the law" (2:15). The only requirement for becoming a Christian was to accept Jesus Christ's message of God's peace and love. Even though they joined in worship, the Gentile newcomers probably had to overcome feelings of alienation before they could feel like established members.

Today, just as it takes time to adjust to a new home, it will also take time for you to adjust to a new congregation, your spiritual home. And the amount of time it takes may vary. Each time I moved, everything around me felt foreign and alien. I felt uncomfortable, like a stranger. Depending on how different my new residence was from my last one, it often took a few weeks, sometimes months, to feel "at home" again. You've probably had these feelings too, and you may even be having them now, as a new member of this church, wondering when you will feel comfortably at home.

When does a newcomer to a church feel like an established member? That's entirely up to you. You might wish to have a formal, external event, like being baptized or confirmed. Perhaps you would feel that you are an "official" member if you are publicly received into the church. Or maybe feeling like an established member will happen when you internally know "here is where I belong." For some new members, it takes a very long time to adjust, to feel like they've spiritually come home. For others, the period may be relatively short. A friend joined a church and attended newcomer activities for three years before feeling comfortable enough to be formally received as a member of the community. I unceremoniously felt right at home in the church I now attend from the very first Sunday I began worshiping there.

Making the transition from being a newcomer to becoming an "established" member may take time, but it is not so much an official occurrence as it is a sense of belonging. No longer feeling like a stranger in your new spiritual home, you're a citizen with the saints, a member of the household of God.

I know not where the road will lead I follow day by day . . . I only know I walk the King's highway.

(*The Hymnal 1982: Hymn 647*)

A new family to our parish conducted an exhaustive four-month search for a new church when the husband was transferred into the area. Because he and his wife were raised in drastically different religious traditions, they sought a compromise denomination. To them, it didn't matter which one they joined, just as long as it had enough common elements from each of their backgrounds to make them both feel comfortable in worshiping together in the same church. During their search, the couple concentrated on attending services of most of the major Christian sects, but they also attended services of smaller, lesser known denominations.

What they discovered, they said, was that "if you strip away the tangible, worldly deviations of how we express our beliefs, all of the different Christian sects are founded upon the same belief in one God. In each and every denomination, we found the same joy in loving and serving Christ."

Just like there is a variety of car makes and models to please different automotive tastes, there are also different denominations to suit various religious and spiritual needs. The denomination you have just decided to join has the same function as any other denomination you might have selected. While religious political structures and physical aspects of the worship service may differ, basic tenets, beliefs, and quests for spiritual fulfillment are the same. By becoming a new member of this church, you have declared yourself to be in the driver's seat of your own spiritual journey. You have just chosen your preferred mode of transportation on the King's highway.

So here you are. It's a time to celebrate. Your new church joyously welcomes you as you begin your spiritual journey toward eternal life. As this hymn suggests, God's path is a great, ineffable, and wondrous mystery. We may not truly know where God's road will lead us, but we surmise and have discovered so far that it brings us closer to God. We are on our way, traveling his highway day by day. Regardless of how we've chosen to travel, we do know that God is with us.

We are on his way together.

Prayers

In Praise of Wisdom
(Wisdom of Sirach 24:19–22)

Come to me, you who desire me, and eat your fill of my fruits. For the memory of me is sweeter than honey, and the possession of me sweeter than honeycomb. Those who eat of me will hunger for more, and those who drink of me will thirst for more. Whoever obeys me will not be put to shame, and those who work with me will not sin.

Dear Lord,
As I become more a part of your community at church, full me with the wisdom of your Holy Spirit to help me with the stresses, weariness, and burdens of my daily life. Keep her presence within me, guiding me so that as I begin to find the fruits of her refreshment within my new parish family, the fruits of my labors will have meaning and purpose. Amen.

Psalm 46

God is our refuge and strength, a very present help in trouble. Therefore we will not fear, though the earth should change, though the mountains shake in the heart of the sea; though its waters roar and foam, though the mountains tremble with its tumult.

There is a river whose streams make glad the city of God, the holy habitation of the Most High. God is in the midst of the city; it shall not be moved; God will help it when the morning dawns. The nations are in an uproar, the kingdoms totter; he utters his voice, the earth melts. The Lord of hosts is with us; the God of Jacob is our refuge.

Come, behold the works of the Lord; see what desolations he has brought on the earth. He makes wars cease to the end of the earth; he breaks the bow, and shatters the spear; he burns the shields with fire. "Be still, and know that I am God! I am exalted among the nations, I am exalted in the earth." The Lord of hosts is with us; the God of Jacob is our refuge.

First New Member's Prayer

Dear Lord,
You've been the inspiration of all the Holy Scriptures, causing them to be written for our learning and understanding. As I begin to study them as a new member of your church, may I wisely begin to realize your eternal love and truth, which is related and revealed in the biblical stories. May I listen to and hear them, reading, studying, marking, and accepting them into my daily life so that I may embrace and hold fast their message of your truth, hope, and promise for everlasting life. Amen.

Second New Member's Prayer

God, this is all new to me, this new church, this new spiritual family. I hope and am praying that I've made the right choice, for myself and others in my life.

As I continue to worship with this congregation, may I find your peace and understanding while in the midst of its members. May I find your solace and eternal grace in the middle of new social activities, within the bustle of seeking acceptance and belonging.

Dear Lord, be ever present alongside of me, so that I might show the new presence of your love growing within me, as I continue upon this new journey as a new member of your community. Amen.

Third New Member's Prayer

I've come out of pain and suffering, God, with heavy burdens and a troubled heart. I am not sure how to ask for your help. No one has taught me to pray. But by coming here and joining this church, perhaps I will learn to pray to you, to talk to you, to have you talk with me. Jesus said that you would help, if only I would ask. I ask now, as a new member of this community, for your help.

Help me to understand and accept what is happening in my life right now. Help me to understand that you have reasons, infinite reasons, and a plan that I cannot understand. Help me to know that in your infinite wisdom what is happening is in my best interests and that, through all this, you are always with me. Amen.

Fourth New Member's Prayer

Dear God,

What a great congregation this is. Thank you for leading me to this place, where so much joy of your love fills up its nave, rooms, and hallways, as well as the hearts of each of its members, who all seem so familiar, sharing with me your joy of being here with us.

Thank you for answering my prayers to find a new church home. Thank you for my meeting so many kind, thoughtful, and considerate members here. Thank you for making them a part of my life and for my becoming a welcomed part of theirs.

Thank you, Lord, for my being here. Amen.

Any Day, Now

Thank you for this new day.
For new beginnings.
For rolling white clouds, swaying thin gray tree boughs,
your whisper sounding lightly in echoes of a rippling creek,
caressing gentle breezes on my cheek,
honest marsh grass hugging under my feet,
my black and tan hound's tags sweetly clinking,
gamboling down soft sandy trails, silence of padded paws,
greens brilliant contrasting blue against yellow rays
warming my soul to its depths
of your being newly growing within me.
A still, quiet moment of silent serenity,
deeply inhaling love,
wondrously exhaling joy.
Thank you for this new day,
and my new beginnings.

From *Exodus Ending* ©1995
June J. McInerney

The Prayer of St. Francis

Lord, make me an instrument of your peace. Where there is hatred, let me sow love; where there is injury, pardon; where there is discord, union; where there is doubt, faith; where there is despair, hope; where there is darkness, light; where there is sadness, joy.

Grant that we may not so much seek to be consoled as to console; to be understood as to understand; to be loved as to love.

For it is in giving that we receive; it is in pardoning that we are pardoned; and it is in dying that we are born to eternal life. Amen.